www.realreads.co.uk

Retold by Alan Moore and Gill Tavner
Illustrated by Karen Donnelly

Published by Real Reads Ltd
Stroud, Gloucestershire, UK
www.realreads.co.uk

ISBN 978-1-906230-27-2

Printed in China by Imago Ltd
Designed by Lucy Guenot
Typeset by Bookcraft Ltd, Stroud, Gloucestershire

CONTENTS

THE CHARACTERS

Mary Magdalene

Jesus brings light into Mary's dark life. How can she help him? What important role will she play?

Sarah

Anxious to help Mary, Sarah invites her to listen to a visiting preacher. Little does she know where this will lead.

Jesus

Jesus wants to show everybody the light that Mary has seen. Why do they find it so difficult to believe him?

Simon Peter

Simon Peter is a true and trusted friend of Jesus. How will he respond to Mary Magdalene when she joins the group?

Judas

Judas is in charge of the disciples' money. How will this affect his relationship with Mary Magdalene?

Pharisees

Insisting upon the Jewish law, these men find Jesus a difficult man to understand.

John

John is one of Jesus's disciples. What important responsibility will he be given?

MARY MAGDALENE

I wonder what people will say about me in the
future. Will they be able to accept that a woman
could be a devoted follower of God's son? Will
they accept the nature of my love for Jesus?

When he was alive, I would have died for
him. Now, a year after his death, I have devoted
my life to spreading his word. Yes – at this
point in history I am free to play this role. I
wonder how history will view this time. How
will it view me?

I grew up in Magdala, on the western shore
of the Sea of Galilee. My parents, devout Jews,
were gentle and loving. They taught me the
scriptures and Jewish laws. All in all, the first
twelve years of my life were very happy years,
unspoilt by any foreboding of what lay ahead.

My happiness ended not long after
my twelfth birthday. My father died of a
sudden illness, leaving me and my mother
heartbroken. In spite of her grief, mother had
to take care of me. Having no money of her
own, she had to remarry. My new stepfather
was an angry and violent man who treated me
and my mother terribly. I feared and hated him.

However, mother had achieved her goal.
He was a wealthy man whose eventual death
when I was twenty-two left us financially
independent.

But what good is money when your
mind and soul are damaged? That was me
throughout my twenties. I was prone to regular
deep depressions in which my mind spiralled
uncontrollably downwards. In those periods,
nothing could lift me. The future seemed dark,
very dark.

I was terrified of men. I tried to avoid company whenever possible, preferring to be alone in my darkness. I hated meeting strangers. I certainly didn't want to accept an invitation to a family wedding in Cana, but my mother insisted. 'You don't have to stay long, Mary. Just show your face. Please.'

Cana is a small town to the west of Magdala. I set off reluctantly, unaware that this was the beginning of a new life – a journey towards light.

After the ceremony, I found a seat in a corner of the feasting room from which I could watch the other guests without attracting any attention to myself. A group of men caught my notice, especially the one called Jesus, who appeared to be the group's leader. Jesus's mother was there too – I watched as he guided her gently into a seat near me. That was what most struck me the first time I saw Jesus – his gentleness.

Jesus and his friends seemed intense but cheerful. They entered into the spirit of the celebrations with great energy, especially one of them, a strong, enthusiastic man. It was he who served food and drink to the others. 'Hey, Simon, could you bring us more wine?' called one of his friends.

'No problem,' he smiled. Simon soon returned, carrying a jug, from which he first served Jesus's mother. She took a sip and leant towards her son. 'This is water. They must

have run out of wine,' I heard her say softly. 'The host will be terribly embarrassed. Can you help him?'

I watched with interest.

'Mother – why involve me?' responded Jesus. 'My time has not yet come.'

She smiled at him. Turning to one of the servants, she quietly advised, 'Do whatever my son tells you.' By now I was fascinated.

Jesus pointed to six large jars. 'Fill those with water,' he told the bemused servants. They did as he asked. 'Now draw some out and take it to the host of the banquet.' One of the servants presented the embarrassed host with a cup filled from one of the jars, pointing to Jesus as he did so.

As soon as the host drank from the cup, a look of wonder brightened his features. For a moment he was stupefied, then his servants swung into action. Soon every pitcher and jug available was being used to fill guests' cups with wine.

A merry guest called out to the host. 'Heh – you sly old thing!' he joked. 'You should have served this wine first. Why did you save the best till now?'

Jesus concentrated on his food, trying to avoid being noticed.

I puzzled for months over what had happened, but found no explanation. It was not until my mother persuaded me to return to Cana to visit the newlyweds that I came across Jesus again and began to understand.

I was in one of my dark periods. Mother thought the change of scene would help. I doubted it, but hadn't the energy to resist.

Fortunately, Sarah, the new wife, was kind and sensitive to my condition, offering me both friendship and space. On my second day there, she suggested gently, 'It might do you good to come out with me this afternoon. A man from Nazareth is preaching in town. He's supposed to be a fantastic speaker.'

'I'm not sure,' I hesitated. 'I don't like crowds.'

'Oh, come on,' she insisted. 'It might be our only chance to hear Jesus.'

'Did you say Jesus?'

Sarah nodded. 'Yes. He was at our wedding.'

It was easy to find Jesus; we just followed the crowd. Sarah had to lead me by the hand as I was afraid to raise my eyes from the ground. I was afraid of people's faces. Panic rose within me as I saw more and more feet, all stirring the dust.

'There he is!' exclaimed Sarah. I couldn't look. I was dizzy, struggling for breath. I pulled against Sarah. 'This way.' Sarah guided me to the side of a house, away from the crowd. We went through the cooler air of the house to the courtyard, where we stood in the doorway just behind Jesus. Here I could breathe more easily.

I recognised Jesus immediately. We were so close that we could almost touch him. Jesus's attention was fixed upon an important-looking man who knelt at his feet. Sarah whispered to me that he was a royal official from Capernaum. 'My son is dying,' he told Jesus.

'Please, come with me to Capernaum. Save him.'

The crowd looked eager. What was Jesus going to do? I wondered whether they would follow him all the way to Capernaum. Jesus looked up from the man with a sigh, and spoke to the people before him. 'You want to see a miracle to prove who I am. Why do you need to see a sign before you believe?'

I wondered what on earth he meant, but the official was more intent on saving his son than in asking questions.

'Please help my child,' he begged.

'Your son lives,' Jesus assured him.

'But won't you come to him?'

'Your son lives,' repeated Jesus.

We learned later that the man's son had recovered at the exact time that Jesus had said those words. The official became a follower of Jesus. I suppose that proved Jesus's point. Would I ever have believed that Jesus was the Son of God without the evidence in Cana, or without what happened to me later that very evening? I don't know.

Two of Sarah's friends invited Jesus to stay in their home. They suggested that Sarah and I dine with them. I was reluctant to accept, but Sarah was keen and I didn't want to disappoint her.

That evening, although I tried to make myself invisible in the shadows, I found myself fascinated by Jesus. Something drew me to him, a force I had never experienced before. I couldn't take my eyes off him, even when he looked in my direction, even when he walked towards me. He sat down beside me, and still I stared. He took my hands in his. 'Mary, you are troubled,' he said gently.

The rest of the room grew silent – or perhaps I just stopped noticing their noise. Jesus seemed aware only of me; nothing else. I started to cry, but I didn't feel embarrassed. Jesus's gaze never left my face; his gentle hands simply held mine tighter.

'Your troubles are in the past,' he whispered. 'Hear my word and believe. I will give you new life.'

Something in the way that he looked at me, giving me his full attention without seeking anything from me, convinced me. My darkness lifted, never to return. This man was truly the light of the world.

'Mary, you seem different,' observed Sarah as we walked home.

'I've changed,' I said, though I wasn't really sure exactly what I meant.

'Mary, you seem different,' observed my mother upon my return to Magdala. I told her everything that had happened. 'I'd like to meet Jesus again,' I concluded, 'but I'm not sure how.'

'You'll find him,' my mother assured me. 'He'll probably be in Jerusalem for the Passover.'

Like most Jews, we always went to Jerusalem to celebrate the Passover. Everyone looked forward to it, and this year, for the first time in many years, so did I.

I wondered how I would possibly find Jesus amongst so many people, but it wasn't difficult. I knew that he now had many followers, so I found a crowd and there he was. Noticing me immediately, he made space for me beside him. 'How are you, Mary?' he asked. He remembered me!

As we walked at the head of the crowd, Jesus explained his mission to create heaven on earth by demonstrating God's love, and clear the way for us all to reach God. I decided that – as much as was possible for a woman – I would follow him and support his work. But I didn't really know how I could do that. What could I offer?

The next morning was the Sabbath. I accompanied Jesus to a pool at Bethesda. Many sick and disabled people visit this pool, hoping to be healed by its waters. Jesus knelt beside a

sorrowful elderly man lying on a mat at the water's edge. 'I have been visiting this pool for thirty-eight years,' explained the man, 'but nobody helps me into the water.'

'If you want to get well,' Jesus told him, 'why don't you pick up your mat and walk?' I watched as the man did just that. 'Now,' said Jesus quite sternly, 'give up your sinful ways, or worse will happen.'

Puzzled by his comment, I asked Jesus what he meant. 'This man's biggest problem isn't his illness. Like all human beings his relationship with God is broken. That is what I have come to mend.'

As I watched the healed man pick his way through the other sick people, I wondered how such brokenness could be fixed. I decided to give everything I had to help Jesus.

I joined Jesus and his followers as often as I could. Some of my friends were scandalised that I travelled with a group of men, but I didn't care what they thought.

My mother understood. We talked for hours about Jesus. I think she was so pleased that my depression had gone, and that the

scars left by my stepfather had healed, that she would have given anything to Jesus in gratitude. 'Use our money to support his mission,' she told me.

At first some of Jesus's friends seemed a little uncomfortable with my presence but, following his example, they gradually accepted me. Simon was perhaps the most welcoming, whilst Judas, in charge of the group's funds, appreciated the important contribution I could make. He seemed pleased, in spite of himself, when some of my wealthy friends also joined us.

On one occasion Simon took us across the Sea of Galilee in his boat, to where a great crowd waited on the opposite shore. Jesus led everybody onto a hillside and began to preach. I watched in wonder as the crowd continued to grow. By the time dusk gathered, there must have been around five thousand people. Five thousand hungry people, I thought to myself.

Judas must have been thinking the same thing. 'Shall we go into the town to buy food?' he suggested, looking to me for support.

'No, we'll feed them now,' replied Jesus. He took what little food we had – five barley loaves and two fish. He gave thanks to God, broke it into pieces, and told us to distribute it among the people. Tentatively, we picked up the baskets he gave us and began to distribute the crumbs. I was  amazed. We all were. The food never ran out. We fed the people until they were satisfied, and still there was more.

That evening Jesus prayed alone, leaving the crowd to wonder at what had happened.

Jesus was often frustrated by people's desperation to see signs and miracles. 'Why?' he once asked me. 'Why do their eyes need to see before their hearts can believe?' But he knew that he had to keep providing signs – even to his closest friends.

After feeding the crowd, Jesus stayed late in the mountains. Simon offered to sail the rest of us back across the water to Capernaum. Thanks to our many trips to and fro over Galilee I was becoming used to sailing, but I can't say I ever felt confident in a boat. That night, the stormy weather and choppy water awakened my old fears. Simon offered to keep watch while we all slept, but I couldn't sleep. 'Don't worry. We'll be fine,' Simon assured me.

Suddenly I spotted something moving towards us over the water, though my eyes were partially blinded by the sea-spray. 'Simon! What's that?' I whispered.

'I don't know,' admitted Simon, wiping water from his own eyes. I was now gripping Simon's arm. Together, we peered into the darkness.

'Don't be afraid.' We heard the familiar voice at the same time as Jesus's features became clear. He walked across the water to us and climbed into the boat. 'Why did you doubt?' he asked calmly.

Some of the crowd left behind on the shore soon found boats to follow us. When they found Jesus already in Capernaum they were puzzled. 'Rabbi, how did you get here?' they asked.

Jesus replied, 'Admit it. You are looking for me because I fed you when you were hungry.' They nodded. 'Believe with your hearts instead of your stomachs. Food rots. Search instead for food that lasts for ever – search for bread for your soul.'

'How can we find such bread?' they asked.

'I bring it from God. This is what I am. Believe in me, the one God has sent.'

'Show us a miracle to help us believe. Do something like Moses did when he fed his people manna in the desert.'

Hadn't Jesus just done exactly that? Why did they keep demanding signs? Why seek answers to their smaller problems rather than their biggest one?

Nevertheless, Jesus replied calmly. 'The

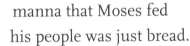

manna that Moses fed his people was just bread. The bread of life is the one that gives life to the world.' People seemed puzzled. Jesus had to spell it out more clearly. 'I am the bread of life. He who comes to me will never go hungry.' Most people still seemed perplexed.

'My friends – you have seen me, and still you doubt! Listen, I have come down from heaven to do my father's will. I am the bread from heaven that you may eat and never die.'

Some people fell to their knees in prayer, but I heard others muttering 'blasphemy'. In spite of hearing Jesus's words and seeing his work, they were still not convinced. One man called out, 'Are you saying you are equal to God?'

Such accusations could result in a person being stoned to death. A shiver ran down my spine. For the first time I felt concerned for Jesus's safety.

I returned home to visit my mother and to replenish my funds, agreeing to meet Jesus and the disciples in Jerusalem a few weeks later. When I returned I brought with me some friends – other women of independent wealth who were keen to support Jesus's work.

We met Jesus in the women's court of the temple. Within minutes, our attention was drawn to something happening in the entrance. We watched as a group of men dragged a distressed woman roughly over the dusty ground. They dropped her at Jesus's feet, where she knelt, weeping. 'Teacher,' one man

explained breathlessly, 'this woman has been with a man other than her husband. Moses commanded us to stone such women. What shall we do?'

I sensed immediately that these men wanted to trap Jesus. If he said that the woman should be released, he would be defying Jewish law. On the other hand his whole message was one of forgiveness. He could not condemn this poor woman to a cruel death by stoning.

Squatting down, Jesus traced patterns in the dust with his finger. I think he was demonstrating his lack of interest in the men's accusations. When they pressed him again for an answer, he looked up at them. 'If any one of you is without sin, let him throw the first stone.' Then he returned his attention to the dust.

The men fell silent. They shuffled their feet uncomfortably. One by one, they drifted away, leaving the accused woman weeping on the ground. I helped her to her feet.

'Stand up,' said Jesus to the woman. 'Who now is here to condemn you?'

She looked around. 'Nobody, Master.'

'And I do not condemn you either. Go now, and sin no more.'

How could such a gentle man make so many enemies? I couldn't understand it, but I saw, with increasing fear, that it was true. I suppose Jesus spoke truths that people did not want to

hear. These people didn't just reject his teaching –
they really hated and feared him. I worried about
him constantly.

Jesus's message was so simple, so peaceful.
He said that we should love God and love each
other. 'I am the light of the world,' he often said.
'Whoever follows me will no longer walk in
darkness, but have eternal life.' He had certainly
replaced my darkness with light, but I don't think
he meant it literally. He meant that he brought us
all a clear view of the way to God.

I particularly remember one occasion when
Jesus outraged his opponents. During his
teaching one day, he said, 'I bring the truth that
will set you free.'

One of the religious leaders was furious.
'But Abraham, the father of the Jewish nation,
freed our people from slavery centuries ago!' he
sputtered. 'You can't set us free! We are not slaves!'

'You are slaves to your sins,' replied Jesus.
'How can you claim to be Abraham's children

when you would kill me for speaking the truth? Abraham wouldn't have done that! You speak the words of the devil, and therefore you are children of the devil.'

I had never experienced such tension. I held my breath.

People's faces were red, their fists clenched. 'We are the children of God! You are the one possessed by the devil!'

'If you were God's children, you would love me and believe what I say.'

'Are you claiming to be greater than Abraham?' they asked.

Jesus looked at them and responded with staggering simplicity. 'Before Abraham was born, I am.' He walked away through the crowd.

I finally breathed again. I felt faint. Had Jesus *really* just told us that he was God, here among us?

Jesus's work never ceased. He still had to provide many signs before people would believe who he was. 'The poor people,' he once sighed when alone with me. 'They are so blind.'

One Sabbath I found Jesus and his disciples outside the temple. They were talking to a blind beggar. As I watched, Jesus gathered some dust and spat on it to make a little mud which he spread over the blind man's eyes. 'Go and wash your eyes in the Pool of Siloam,' he directed.

When the man had left, Jesus told us, 'As long as I am here I must do God's work. For this short time that I am in the world, I must help people to see.'

Later, Judas and I went to buy food for the others. 'I wonder what happened to that blind man?' mused Judas. He was soon answered when we noticed a small crowd, at the centre of which we saw the man talking with great excitement. 'Honestly!' he cried, 'When I washed the mud from my eyes at Siloam, I could see! I can see you all now – you, who know that I've been blind since birth!'

The amazed crowd didn't know how to act. 'We should take him to see the Pharisees,' they decided. 'They'll know what to do.'

'Let's follow,' Judas whispered to me.

The Pharisees looked distinctly uncomfortable when they heard the man's story. 'Jesus can't be from God,' they declared, after some thought, 'because he broke God's law by healing you on the Sabbath!'

'But he must be from God. How else could he make a blind man see?' responded one man in the crowd. He turned to the healed man. 'It was your eyes he opened. What do you say about him?'

'I was blind, but now I can see,' was his simple

reply. 'I've already told you what happened. How can you possibly doubt who Jesus is? He must be from God to have done this.'

His impatience enraged the Pharisees. 'This man is pretending. He must be working for Jesus.' They knew that they would have to discredit the man to stop the crowd believing him. 'You were blind from your birth,' they shouted. 'Blindness is a punishment for sin! How dare you, a sinner, lecture us?'

Judas drew the healed man away from the crowd. 'Come with us,' he said softly. 'We'll take you back to Jesus.'

Of course, Jesus welcomed him with open arms. 'Do you believe in the Son of God?' he asked.

'Who is he, Master? Tell me, so that I can believe in him.'

'You see me now before you,' replied Jesus. 'I have come into this world so that the blind will see.'

The man fell to his knees. 'Lord, I believe!'

Jesus truly loved everybody, even those who opposed him. He likened himself to a good shepherd. A good shepherd, he told us, would lay down his life for his flock. This filled me with dread. I had no doubt at all that Jesus would be prepared to lay down his life for his flock if he had to. His love for others was pure and selfless; it never failed him, whatever the test.

Of course, Jesus had some particularly close friends in addition to those of us who followed him. Whenever we were in Bethany, we visited the sisters Mary and Martha and their brother, Lazarus. I formed a close friendship with Martha. She was a very practical woman. One day Jesus heard from Martha that Lazarus was dangerously ill.

'We should go now,' I urged. 'Martha wouldn't trouble you unless she was really worried.'

'We'll complete our work here first,' Jesus replied.

My head told me that I had to trust Jesus, but the tightness in my stomach matched the fear I felt.

Two days later Jesus gathered us all together. 'Our friend Lazarus has died,' he told us. 'We must go to him.' How did he know?

By the time we reached Bethany, Lazarus had been dead for four days. Dressed in black, Martha emerged from her house. When she hugged me, I felt her trembling. She turned to Jesus, tears in her eyes. 'Lord, if you had come earlier Lazarus wouldn't have died.'

Jesus held her close to him. 'Martha, I am the resurrection and the life. Whoever believes in me will never die. Do you believe this?'

'Yes, Lord.'

'Lazarus will rise again.'

'I know that he'll rise to heaven, Lord, but we want him here with us.'

Her sister Mary emerged from the house and sank to her knees before Jesus. Her words echoed Martha's. 'Lord, if you had been here Lazarus would still be alive.'

Moved by their distress, Jesus asked them to lead us to Lazarus's tomb. When we arrived, Simon helped him to move aside the huge stone sealing the entrance. Jesus prayed. 'Father, thank you for hearing me. Let these people see and believe.' Then he called, 'Lazarus, come out!'

We held our breath and stared at the hole in the rock. There was a shuffling sound. A slight movement. I gasped as Lazarus walked from the tomb. His strong, healthy body was still wrapped in his burial shroud.

Not even death could defeat Jesus.

Bethany was close to Jerusalem, so Mary, Martha and Lazarus were able to update us with news from the city. The ever-increasing number of people believing that Jesus was the Son of God was making both the Romans and the Jewish leaders nervous. 'The Pharisees have asked the Sanhedrin to find a way to stop you,' Lazarus warned Jesus. The Sanhedrin was the governing council, and held a great deal of power. 'The high priest has said that it's better for one good man to die than for the whole Jewish nation to perish.'

'It's too soon,' said Jesus quietly. 'We will go away to the desert, to Ephraim. We'll come back in time for the Passover.'

'I'll stay here with our friends and await your return,' I said.

We knew that Jesus would keep his word. When the time came for his return, Martha and I prepared a special meal. Mary took all her savings and went to buy perfume to anoint Jesus. I understood her desire – her concerns were always more spiritual than those of her sister.

Crowds gathered outside the house. Word of Lazarus's resurrection had spread far and wide, and people were eager to see both men. That night, at dinner, Jesus warned Lazarus. 'The crowds bring danger. You should keep a low profile until I am gone.'

'Gone, Lord?' asked Mary. Then, weeping, she poured her expensive perfume over Jesus's feet.

Jesus noticed Judas's shocked expression. 'Judas, you think Mary should have given her money to the poor, don't you? The poor will always be amongst you, but you will not always have me. Mary's gift prepares me for my burial.'

The following day Jesus rode into Jerusalem.
Martha and I had gone ahead. As Jesus
approached we joined the crowds lining the
streets, waving palm branches and shouting.
Our scriptures had told us that our king would
enter Jerusalem on a donkey and that we

shouldn't be afraid. I tried not to think about what the scriptures said would happen next.

That night, Jesus invited his disciples to share their last meal together. It was traditional that only men should attend such meals, so I stayed with Mary and Martha. It wasn't until after Jesus's death that Simon told me about that night's terrible events.

'Jesus washed our feet!' exclaimed Simon. 'I objected, but he said I had to let him wash me or I was no part of him. He told us to serve others as he served us. After the meal,' continued Simon more quietly, 'he said that one of us would betray him.'

'I know,' I sighed sadly. 'The others told me when they returned to Bethany. They told me about everything Judas did.'

'How could he do it, Mary?' Simon broke down in tears. 'How could Judas betray Jesus?'

Simon fell silent. I placed my hand on his shoulder, but he shrugged it off. 'I don't deserve your sympathy, Mary. I too have betrayed Jesus.'

'Simon, surely you're the last person on earth who would ... '

'Oh, Mary!' he interrupted me. 'I followed when they arrested him. They took him to the high priest's house. I watched them whip him. I watched his skin being torn from his body.' Simon's hands covered his eyes, as though trying to shield them from the terrible things he had seen. 'Such pain!'

I tried to comfort him. 'You couldn't have helped.'

'It's worse that that, Mary. I was so scared.' He paused and took a deep, trembling breath before he continued. 'I denied him three times, Mary. That night I told three people that I didn't know Jesus.'

I put my arms around him as he sobbed. 'Jesus would understand,' I soothed. 'You were afraid for your life.'

'My life is now his,' he resolved. 'I'll devote my remaining years to him. I will die for him.'

'I'm sure you will,' I answered. That wasn't exactly what I meant to say.

None of us slept on the night of Jesus's arrest. Early the next morning, John set out to search for Jesus's mother. She would be in Jerusalem for the Passover, and would be in need of comfort. I decided to try to find Jesus.

Arriving in the city, I heard the news that Jesus was to be crucified that day. Crucifixion – an agonising death on a cross – was the most terrible death imaginable. My knees collapsed beneath me. Only my determination to find Jesus gave me strength.

To find Jesus I did as I had always done – I followed the crowds. Bent low under the immense weight of a beam of wood, Jesus was barely recognisable. His body was broken and bruised, with open lacerations and dried blood. Flies buzzed around him. Soldiers were forcing him to carry his own cross to Golgotha, the place of crucifixion. Shocked, I joined a group of women following him.

Progress was so slow. Jesus stumbled often, and I ached to help him. At one point I noticed John in the crowd at the side of the road. Next to him stood Jesus's mother. John supported her weight as she watched her son pass by.

How can I find words to describe Jesus's crucifixion? I can only tell what I saw. Soldiers had nailed a sign above his head, saying 'The King of the Jews'. They wanted to humiliate him. They had pushed a crown of thorns on his head, from which blood still ran down his face. At the foot of his cross, where I knelt with Mary and John, soldiers gambled for the clothes they had taken from him.

Jesus looked down at his mother and John. 'Mother, this is your son,' he said. 'John, this is your mother. Care for her.'

His suffering was long and terrible. Near the end Jesus said 'I am thirsty.' Soldiers soaked a sponge in wine vinegar and put it to his lips. I could tell that he was praying. His eyes were closed but his lips were moving. He opened his eyes for one last time to look upon the world he so loved. With his final breath, he said, 'It is finished.'

Towards dusk, soldiers broke the legs of those being crucified who were still alive, so they could not press down on their feet and would suffocate more quickly. As Jesus appeared to be dead already, they pushed a spear into his side to be sure. Blood and water ran out.

We wept as they brought Jesus's body down from his cross. Joseph of Arimathea, an influential Jew and a secret follower of Jesus, arranged for Jesus's body to be buried in his own tomb.

The next morning, after another sleepless night, I arose before daybreak and walked to the tomb. It had been cut out of the rock and, like Lazarus's tomb, it had a stone across the entrance. Or at least it should have had. I stopped and stared in disbelief. The stone had been rolled back. The tomb was open. Dreading the sight that would greet me, I crept towards the opening and peered in. It was empty!

I don't know how to describe my feelings at that moment. Horror? Relief? Excitement? I turned and ran to the house in which Simon and John were looking after Mary. 'Simon!' I hammered on the door. 'Simon!'

He appeared. He looked exhausted.

'They've taken his body out of the tomb! I don't know where they've put him!'

Simon and John ran. I followed. I found them talking excitedly outside the tomb. I looked inside again, more calmly this time. I noticed that the burial clothes were neatly folded.

'We need to tell the others,' said Simon.

'I'll stay here.' I felt unable to leave. In a dreamlike state, I felt compelled to look in the tomb again. This time, I saw two beings dressed in white – they must have been angels – seated where the body had been.

'Why are you crying?' one of them asked.

'They have taken my Lord away, and I don't know where they've put him.'

The angels' eyes focused upon something behind me. A shiver ran down my spine as I turned, afraid of what I might see.

My eyes were blurred with tears. That's my only excuse for failing to recognise him – I suppose it's a feeble one. I thought it was the gardener. 'Why are you crying?' he asked. 'Who are you looking for?'

'Sir,' I wept, 'please tell me where you've put him.'

'Mary,' answered the man. I knew that voice.

'Rabboni!' I cried, 'Teacher!'

I threw myself towards him, but he stepped back.

'Do not reach for me now, for I have not yet returned to the father,' he explained. 'Go and tell the others that I am returning to my father.'

That evening we gathered together in secret.
As Jesus's friends, our lives were in danger.
Only one of our close group was missing –
Thomas. We were all concerned for his safety.

The fear and tension in the room suddenly
eased into an unexpected sense of calm. Jesus
appeared in our midst, just as he had appeared
to me outside his tomb. 'Peace be with you,'
he said gently. 'Understand this. I had to take
on the world's sins and clear the way to God
by dying and living again. Now, as the father
sent me, I am sending you.' Then he breathed
on us. 'Receive the Holy Spirit,' he explained.
'If you forgive anyone their sins, those sins
are forgiven.' While we all considered the
enormity of his words, he disappeared from
our sight.

A knock on the door announced Thomas's
arrival. When we told him that Jesus had
been there he looked hurt. 'Why do you say
this? Why are you lying to me?' No matter

how much we protested, he would not be convinced. 'Unless I see the nail marks in his hands and put my fingers into his wounds,' he said, 'I will not believe it.'

A week later we had all gathered in the same room. This time, Thomas was with us. Once again, we felt Jesus's calming presence. Thomas was wide-eyed. Jesus walked towards him, holding out his wounded hands. 'Put your fingers in my wounds, Thomas. Put your

hand in my side. Never doubt again.'

Thomas did as Jesus had invited and fell to his knees. 'My Lord and my God!'

'Thomas,' said Jesus, laying a hand upon his shoulder. 'You believe because you have seen me. Blessed are those who believe without needing to see me.'

I remember again the question Jesus once asked me. 'Why do people need to see before they can believe?'

We have all seen. Whether or not we would have believed without seeing is a question we often discuss, a question none of us can answer.

One thing, however, is certain. We are the lucky few. Our work now is to tell our story, so that other people might hear about Jesus. It will be more difficult for them, for you. We have to tell it in such a way that people will be able to believe without having to see.

This is how I will spend the rest of my life.

TAKING THINGS FURTHER
The real read

This *Real Reads* volume of *Mary Magdalene* is our interpretation of the events of the New Testament, told from the perspective of one of its most enigmatic and, recently, controversial participants. In writing this account of Mary Magdalene's life, we have used evidence from the gospel according to John. This is one of the four gospels – the first four books of the New Testament.

It is important to acknowledge that all four gospels were written after Jesus's death, and that the writers had different aims in mind – although they all wanted to engender faith in the reader that Jesus was the Son of God. The first three gospels – Matthew, Mark and Luke – are called 'the synoptic gospels'. They were probably written between forty and sixty years after the crucifixion. The gospel according to John, written later, is significantly different.

Sometimes, the four gospels' accounts of events differ considerably. At first this made our task rather difficult, until we realised that what we needed to do was present the New Testament as it is, rather than to weave a path of our choice between the gospels. Therefore, if you read all six books in the *Real Reads* New Testament series, you may well notice some of the apparent contradictions and inconsistencies that are present in the Bible itself.

In writing each of the six *Real Reads* New Testament books we chose a specific source to follow. To write Mary's account of her life we decided to use John's gospel, because it provides the most information about Mary. However, even in this gospel there is not a great deal of information. For *Mary Magdalene*, perhaps more than any of the other books in this series, we have had to add material from our own imaginations. Nevertheless, we have tried very hard to stay close to the New Testament evidence.

This *Real Reads Mary Magdalene* does not cover all the events of the New Testament.

Reading the other five books in the series will bring you closer to an understanding of the complete story. You may then want to read the New Testament itself. We recommend that you read either the *New International Version* or *The Youth Bible*, details of which are given below.

Biblical sources

Although *Mary Magdalene* is based on the story as told in the gospel of John, there are a few places where we have drawn on other sources.

On the *Real Reads* website you will find an online concordance (www.realreads.co.uk/ newtestament/concordance/marymagdalene). A 'bible concordance' is an indexing tool which allows you to see how the same words, sentences and passages appear in different versions and translations of the Bible. This online concordance will direct you from events in the *Real Reads* version back to their biblical sources, so you can see clearly where each part of our story is drawn from.

Life in
New Testament times

The main events of Mary Magdalene's life took place in Palestine, a long narrow area of land bordered to the west by the Mediterranean Sea and to the east by the Transjordanian Desert. Some parts of Palestine were desert, some were hill country, some rich pasture land, and some uncultivated wilderness. Mary was probably born in Magdala, on the western shore of Lake Galilee, an area with a mixed population of Jews and Gentiles, and a reputation for political unrest. She was probably from a wealthy family and she had wealthy friends.

Although Palestine was Jewish land, it was part of the Roman Empire and under Roman control. The Jews resented paying taxes to Rome. During Jesus's lifetime, there was considerable conflict between the Jews and their Roman rulers. This helps to explain why the Romans might have been nervous of the crowds following Jesus. It also helps to explain

N
W · E
S

Capernaum •

SEA
OF
GALILEE

Cana •

Magdala •

GALILEE

Nazareth •

PALESTINE

RIVER JORDAN

Ephraim •

Jerusalem •

Bethany •

0   10   20 miles

DEAD
SEA

why Mary often felt nervous about Jesus's safety.

You may notice that more women appear in *Real Reads Mary Magdalene* than in the other books in the series. These days, we assume that women played a very minor role in political life during Jesus's times, but that is not necessarily true. Many people accept that, over the centuries, women's roles in the story of Jesus have been significantly reduced. Mary could very well have been a leading member of the early church.

A great many things have been written about Mary Magdalene, and you may find it rewarding to research them further. You can decide for yourself which theory is most likely to be true.

Finding out more

We recommend the following books and websites to gain a greater understanding of the New Testament.

Books

We strongly recommend that you read the rest of the *Real Reads* New Testament series, as the six narratives interlock to give a more complete picture of events. These are *Jesus of Nazareth, Mary of Galilee, Simon Peter, Judas Iscariot,* and *Paul of Tarsus.*

- *New Century Youth Bible*, Authentic Lifestyle, 2007.

- *People in the Life of Jesus*, Colin Lumsden, Day One Publications, 2003. A colouring book.

- Sara Hartman, *Mary Magdalene's Easter Story*, Concordia, 2005.

- Mildred Tuck, *A Child's Book of Miracles and Wonders*, Standard Publishing, 2003.

Websites

- www.bbc.co.uk/religion/religions/
christianity/history/marymagdalene.shtml
Lots of information about Mary Magdalene.

- www.magdalene.org
A useful site – targeted at adults, but with a short introduction to Mary Magdalene and some helpful links.

TV and film

- *Jesus of Nazareth*, directed by Franco Zeffirelli, ITV DVD, 1977. A six and a half hour mini-series.

- *The Miracles of Jesus*, Boulevard Entertainment, 2006. A short animated film.

- *Jesus Christ Superstar*, directed by Norman Jewison, Universal Pictures UK, 2005. This screen version of the 1970s rock opera by Tim Rice and Andrew Lloyd Webber focuses on Jesus's final days, but pays more attention to his relationship with Judas than to his relationship with Mary Magdalene.

Food for thought

Here are some things to think about if you are reading *Mary Magdalene* alone, and ideas for discussion if you are reading it with friends.

Starting points

- How many references can you find to darkness and light? Why do you think Mary calls Jesus 'the light of the world'?

- How does Mary decide to help Jesus? How important do you think this is?

- Make a list of the miracles Mary witnesses. What do you think a miracle is, and why do you think some people need to see them?

- Why do you think Jesus is saddened by people's need to experience miracles?

- Choose one of the miracles described in the book, and retell the story through the eyes of the person Jesus helped.

- Jesus describes himself in several ways – the good shepherd, the bread of life, and the light of the world. Choose one of these, and try to explain what you think he means.

- Many people have suggested that Mary and Jesus were married. If that had been true, how much do you think it would have changed the story?

- Mary is the first person to see the risen Christ. Some people think this makes her the first Christian. What do you think?

Group activities

- Together, make a list of all the references to women in this book. What roles do the different women play? How are they treated?

- With one person as a reporter, the others in the group can play the roles of the disciples, including Simon Peter and Judas. The reporter asks the disciples what they thought about Mary joining the group. Did their feelings change as time went on?

- Talk in the group about miracles. Do you believe in them? Do you think there are miracles in everyday life today?

- At the end of her story, Mary wonders whether she would have believed what had happened without seeing it for herself. Christians all over the world today believe the story without seeing it. Discuss with your group whether it is easy to believe things without having first-hand proof. Create a list of things you all believe without actually seeing any evidence – if there are any!